THE LITTLE BOOK OF

RESILIENCE

Parts of this book were first published in 2020 by Trigger, an imprint of Shaw Callaghan Ltd.

This expanded edition published in 2023 by OH! an Imprint of Welbeck Non-Fiction Limited, part of Welbeck Publishing Group.
Offices in: London – 20 Mortimer Street, London W1T 3JW
and Sydney – 205 Commonwealth Street, Surry Hills 2010
www.welbeckpublishing.com

Compilation text © Welbeck Non-Fiction Limited 2023
Design © Welbeck Non-Fiction Limited 2023

Disclaimer:

ISBN 978-1-80069-356-2

Editorial: Victoria Denne
Project manager: Russell Porter
Production: Jess Brisley

A CIP catalogue record for this book is available from the British Library

Printed in China

10 9 8 7 6 5 4 3 2 1

THE LITTLE BOOK OF
RESILIENCE

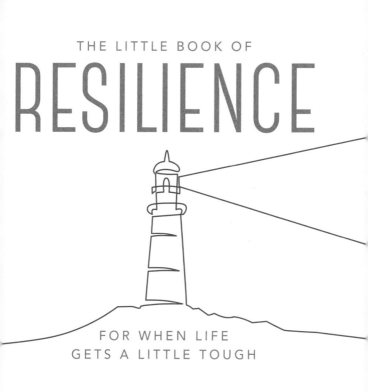

FOR WHEN LIFE
GETS A LITTLE TOUGH

CONTENTS

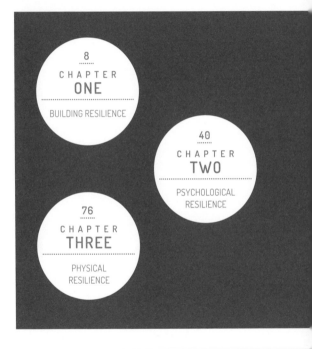

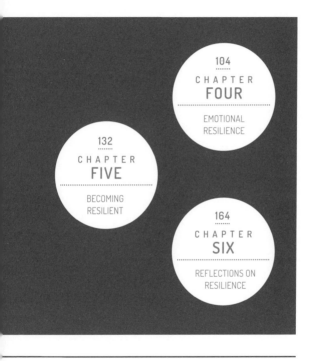

INTRODUCTION

Resilience is something that's a little hard to define and almost impossible to quantify. Whether physical, psychological or emotional, it can be difficult to cultivate within ourselves. However, the rewards of strong resilience to our mental and physical wellbeing are immeasurable.

The Little Book of Resilience offers thought-provoking commentary from some of the world's greatest minds in the art of building resilience to better equip us for crisis and adversity. As you'll soon discover, even a little resilience can go a long way in helping us cope during challenging times.

CHAPTER

1

BUILDING RESILIENCE

Build mental, emotional and behavioural flexibility in order to improve your resilience to adversity and bounce back despite challenging circumstances.

It's not the absence of fear.
It's overcoming it. Sometimes you've
got to blast through and have faith.

Emma Watson

Part of being optimistic is keeping one's head pointed toward the sun, one's feet moving forward. There were many dark moments when my faith in humanity was sorely tested but I would not and could not give myself up to despair.

Nelson Mandela

Life is like riding a bicycle: to keep your
balance you must keep moving.

Albert Einstein

66

If you're walking down the right path
and you're willing to keep walking,
eventually you'll make progress.

Barack Obama

You can rise up from anything.
You can completely recreate
yourself. Nothing is permanent.
You're not stuck. You have
choices. You can think new
thoughts. You can learn

something new. You can create
new habits. All that matters
is that you decide today and
never look back.

Idil Ahmed

66

It's a journey, and the sad thing is you only learn from experience: so as much as someone can tell you things you have to go out there and make your own mistakes in order to learn.

Emma Watson

I've never walked away from
anything – and I'm not going
to start now.

Karren Brady

66

Someone was hurt before you,
wronged before you, hungry before
you, frightened before you, beaten
before you, humiliated before you,

raped before you yet, someone survived. You can do anything you choose to do.

Maya Angelou

It's a slow process, but
quitting won't speed it up.

Anonymous

There's no shame in failing.
The only shame is not giving
things your best shot.

Robin Williams

"

To be rendered powerless does
not destroy your humanity. Your
resilience is your humanity. The
only people who lose their humanity
are those who believe they have

the right to render another human
being powerless. They are the
weak. To yield and not break, that is
incredible strength.

Hannah Gadsby

**Life may try to knock you down
but be persistent with your passions
and cultivate grit, resilience, tenacity
and endurance, success will come.**

Amit Ray

I realized that I don't have to be
perfect. All I have to do is show up
and enjoy the messy imperfect and
beautiful journey of my life.

Kerry Washington

Our greatest glory is not in never falling,
but in rising every time we fall.

Confucius

66

The oak fought the wind and was
broken, the willow bent when it
must and survived.

Robert Jordan

Hold yourself responsible
for a higher standard than
anybody else expects of you.
Never excuse yourself.

Never pity yourself. Be a hard master to yourself – and be lenient to everybody else.

Henry Ward Beecher

Persistence and resilience only
come from having been given
the chance to work through
difficult problems.

Gever Tulley

It's your reaction to adversity, not adversity itself that determines how your life's story will develop.

Dieter F. Uchtdorf

Do not judge me by my success,
judge me by how many times I fell
down and got back up again.

Nelson Mandela

I can be changed by what happens to me. But I refuse to be reduced by it.

Maya Angelou

On the other side of a storm
is the strength that comes from
having navigated through it.
Raise your sail and begin.

Gregory S. Williams

Only those who dare to fail greatly,
can ever achieve greatly.

Robert F. Kennedy

66

Forget mistakes. Forget failures.
Forget everything except what you
are going to do right now, and do it.
Today is your lucky day.

Will Durant

Fall seven times, stand up eight.

Japanese proverb

If you're going through
hell, keep going.

Winston Churchill

Courage doesn't always roar.
Sometimes courage is the quiet
voice at the end of the day saying,
'I will try again tomorrow'.

Mary Anne Radmacher

CHAPTER

2

PSYCHOLOGICAL RESILIENCE

By exhibiting psychological resilience, such as adapting to uncertainty and remaining calm during a crisis, we can protect ourselves from the potential long-term negative consequences of trauma and adversity.

If you think you are too small
to make a difference, try
sleeping with a mosquito.

Dalai Lama

The greatest test of courage
on Earth is to bear defeat
without losing heart.

Robert Green Ingersoll

However difficult life may seem,
there is always something you
can do and succeed at.

Stephen Hawking

People who wonder whether
the glass is half empty
or half full miss the point.
The glass is refillable.

Anonymous

You can go a month without food, you can live three days without water, but you can't go more than sixty seconds without hope.

Sean Swarner

Only you and you alone can change your situation. Don't blame it on anything or anyone.

Leonardo DiCaprio

If I cannot do great things,
I can do small things in a great way.

Martin Luther King Jr.

All the people who knock me down,
only inspire me to do better.

Selena Gomez

Whatever words we utter should
be chosen with care, for people
will hear them and be influenced
by them... for good or ill.

Buddha

We must be willing to let go of the
life we planned so as to have the
life that is waiting for us.

Joseph Campbell

First principle: never to let one's self be beaten down by persons or by events.

Marie Curie

The thing you fear most has no power.
Your fear of it is what has the power.
Facing the truth really will set you free.

Oprah Winfrey

66

I count him braver who overcomes
his desires than him who conquers
his enemies for the hardest victory
is over the self.

Aristotle

To be nobody but yourself in a world that's doing its best to make you somebody else is to fight the hardest battle you are ever going to fight. Never stop fighting.

E. E. Cummings

Life opens up opportunities to you, and you either take them or you stay afraid of taking them.

Jim Carrey

We ourselves feel that we are a drop in the ocean. But the ocean would be less because of that missing drop.

Mother Teresa

The only way to make sense out of
change is to plunge into it, move
with it, and join the dance.

Alan Watts

One's dignity may be assaulted,
vandalized and cruelly mocked,
but it can never be taken away
unless it is surrendered.

Michael J. Fox

66

My scars remind me that I did indeed
survive my deepest wounds. That in
itself is an accomplishment. And they
bring to mind something else, too.
They remind me that the damage
life has inflicted on me has, in many

places left me stronger and more resilient. What hurt me in the past has actually made me better equipped to face the present.

Steve Goodier

Learn what is to be taken
seriously and laugh at the rest.

Herman Hesse

Turn your wounds into wisdom.

Oprah Winfrey

Sometimes, carrying on,
just carrying on, is the
superhuman achievement.

Albert Camus

It's a funny thing about life, once you
begin to take note of the things you
are grateful for, you begin to lose
sight of the things that you lack.

Germany Kent

Like tiny seeds with potent power to push through tough ground and become mighty trees, we hold innate reserves of unimaginable strength. We are resilient.

Catherine DeVrye

Failure will never overtake me
if my determination to succeed
is strong enough.

Og Mandino

I hope you never fear those
mountains in the distance.
Never settle for the path of
least resistance.

Lee Ann Womack

Resilience is knowing that you are the only one that has the power and the responsibility to pick yourself up.

Mary Holloway

The human capacity for burden is like bamboo – far more flexible than you'd ever believe at first glance.

Jodi Picoult

It's your reaction to adversity, not
adversity itself that determines
how your life's story will develop.

Dieter F. Uchtdorf

No one escapes pain, fear, and suffering. Yet from pain can come wisdom, from fear can come courage, from suffering can come

strength – if we have the
virtue of resilience.

Eric Greitens

No matter how bleak or menacing
a situation may appear, it does
not entirely own us. It can't take
away our freedom to respond, our
power to take action.

Ryder Carroll

When we learn how to become
resilient, we learn how to embrace
the beautifully broad spectrum of
the human experience.

Jaeda Dewalt

CHAPTER
3

PHYSICAL RESILIENCE

By developing a strong physical resilience, we equip our bodies with the stamina to adapt to physical challenges. This also enables us to sustain periods of intense physical stress, such as injury or illness, and recover quickly and efficiently.

“

Only a man who knows what it is like
to be defeated can reach down to the
bottom of his soul and come up with
the extra ounce of power it takes to
win when the match is even.

Muhammad Ali

Resilience isn't a single skill.
It's a variety of skills and coping
mechanisms. To bounce back
from bumps in the road as well
as failures, you should focus on
emphasizing the positive.

Jean Chatzky

Sometimes, things may not go
your way, but the effort should
be there every single night.

Michael Jordan

Out of suffering have emerged the
strongest souls; the most massive
characters are seared with scars.

Kahlil Gibran

Success isn't always about 'greatness', it's about consistency. Consistent, hard work gains success. Greatness will come.

Dwayne "The Rock" Johnson

It is better to risk starving to death
than surrender. If you give up on
your dreams, what's left?

Jim Carrey

The strongest oak of the forest is not the one that is protected from the storm and hidden from the sun. It's the one that stands in the open

where it is compelled to struggle for
its existence against the winds and
rains and the scorching sun.

Napoleon Hill

It may sound strange,
but many champions are made
champions by setbacks.

Bob Richards

It's not stress that kills us; it is our reaction to it. Adopting the right attitude can convert a negative stress into a positive one.

Hans Selye

We all have battles to fight. And it's often in those battles that we are most alive: it's on the frontlines of our lives that we earn wisdom,

create joy, forge friendships,
discover happiness, find love, and
do purposeful work.

Eric Greitens

The difference between a strong
man and a weak one is that the former
does not give up after a defeat.

Woodrow Wilson

I don't count my sit-ups. I only start counting once it starts hurting.

Muhammad Ali

There's no glory in climbing a mountain if all you want to do is to get to the top. It's experiencing the climb itself – in all its moments of

revelation, heartbreak, and fatigue
– that has to be the goal.

Karyn Kusama

If you fail to prepare,
you're prepared to fail.

Mark Spitz

Never let your head hang down.
Never give up and sit down and
grieve. Find another way.

Satchel Paige

"

Climb if you will, but remember that
courage and strength are nought
without prudence, and that a
momentary negligence may destroy
the happiness of a lifetime.

Do nothing in haste; look well
to each step; and from the
beginning think what may be.

Edward Whymper

Everyone wants to live on top
of the mountain, but all the
happiness and growth occurs
while you're climbing it.

Andy Rooney

It's not whether you get knocked down; it's whether you get up.

Vince Lombardi

Never say never because limits, like
fears, are often just an illusion.

Michael Jordan

Run when you can, walk if
you have to, crawl if you must;
just never give up.

Dean Karnazes

The summit is what drives us, but the climb itself is what matters.

Conrad Anker

I just knew if it could be done, it had
to be done, and I did it.

Gertrude Ederle

CHAPTER

4

EMOTIONAL RESILIENCE

Emotional resilience allows us to understand and process our emotional responses. It shapes how we manage extreme emotions and external stressors and enables us to tap into realistic optimism even when faced with a crisis.

If your heart is broken,
make art with the pieces.

Shane Koyczan

I went through a long period where
I was afraid of doing things I wanted
to do, and you get your courage back,
which is what's important.

George Michael

Resilience is not what happens
to you. It's how you react to,
respond to, and recover from
what happens to you.

Jeffrey Gitomer

The presence of evil was something to be first recognized, then dealt with, survived, outwitted, triumphed over.

Toni Morrison

You have to stop crying, and
you have to go kick some ass.

Lady Gaga

Do not pray for an easy life,
pray for the strength to
endure a difficult one.

Bruce Lee

Tragedy should be utilized as a source of strength. No matter what sort of difficulties, how painful experience is, if we lose our hope, that's our real disaster.

Dalai Lama

Remember that sometimes,
not getting what you want is
a wonderful stroke of luck.

Dalai Lama

It's only a bad day, not a bad life.

Anonymous

My barn having burned down, I
can now see the moon.

Mizuta Masahide

All those things that you're worried about are not important. You're going to be OK. Better than OK. You're going to be great. Spend less time tearing yourself apart, worrying if you're good enough. You are good enough. And you're going to meet amazing people in your life who will help you and love you.

Reese Witherspoon

Live to the point of tears.

Albert Camus

We are healed from suffering only by experiencing it to the full.

Marcel Proust

The best people possess a feeling for beauty, the courage to take risks, the discipline to tell the truth, the capacity for sacrifice. Ironically, their virtues

make them vulnerable;
they are often wounded,
sometimes destroyed.

Ernest Hemingway

Never be ashamed of a scar;
it simply means you were stronger
than whatever tried to hurt you.

Demi Lovato

Every morning we are born again. What we do today is what matters most.

Buddha

"

There comes a time in your life when you walk away from all the drama and people who create it. You surround yourself with people who make you laugh. Forget the bad and focus on the good. Love the people who treat you right, pray for the ones who do not. Life is too short to be anything but happy. Falling down is a part of life, getting back up is living.

José N. Harris

A man can only do what he
can do. But if he does that
each day he can sleep at night
and do it again the next day.

Albert Schweitzer

A clay pot sitting in the sun will always be a clay pot. It has to go through the white heat of the furnace to become porcelain.

Mildred Witte Stouven

I am not afraid of storms, for
I am learning to sail my ship.

Louisa May Alcott

Instead of seeing the rug being
pulled from under us, we can learn
to dance on the shifting carpet.

Thomas Crum

Truly, it is in the darkness that one finds
the light, so when we are in sorrow,
then this light is nearest of all to us.

Meister Eckhart

66

Life can only be understood backwards,
it has to be lived forwards.

Soren Kierkegaard

CHAPTER

5

BECOMING RESILIENT

Sometimes life feels like a battlefield, but when you have the benefit of strong psychological, physical and emotional resilience, if you stumble and fall you can quickly regain control and move forward in a healthy and positive way.

A hero is an ordinary individual
who finds the strength to
persevere and endure in spite of
overwhelming obstacles.

Christopher Reeve

If the fire in your heart is strong
enough, it will burn away any
obstacles that come your way.

Suzy Kassem

I am the underdog, and I want to prove that one can follow one's dreams despite all the flaws and setbacks.

Winnie Harlow

Falling down is an accident.
Staying down is a choice.

Rosemary Nonny Knight

Be true to your heart ... put your whole heart and soul into it, and then whatever you do, it will shine through.

Jamie Brewer

We fall. We break. We fail. But then,
we rise. We heal. We overcome.

Kiana Azizian

Hate no one, no matter how much they've wronged you. Live humbly, no matter how wealthy you become. Think positively, no matter how hard life is. Give much, even if you've been given little. Forgive all, especially yourself. And never stop praying for the best for everyone.

Imam

You'll never do a whole lot
unless you're brave enough to try.

Dolly Parton

I allow myself to fail.
I allow myself to break.
I'm not afraid of my flaws.

Lady Gaga

Resilience is accepting your new reality, even if it's less good than the one you had before. You can fight it, you can do nothing but scream about what you've lost or you can accept that and try to put together something that's good.

Elizabeth Edwards

Only those who dare to fail greatly,
can ever achieve greatly.

Robert F. Kennedy

It's during our very worst fall that
we can either die or learn to fly.

Sira Masetti

I just feel like there is
nothing I cannot do.

Stormzy

You've got enemies?
Good; that means you actually
stood up for something.

Winston Churchill

There's no such thing as
ruining your life. Life's a pretty
resilient thing, it turns out.

Sophie Kinsella

Resiliency is something you do, more than something you have You become highly resilient by continuously learning your best way of being yourself in your circumstance.

Al Siebert

Sometimes you just
gotta let shit go and say
'To hell with it' and move on.

Eminem

Change what you can,
manage what you can't.

Raymond McCauley

"

Everyone has the ability to increase resilience to stress. It requires hard work and dedication, but over time, you can equip yourself to handle whatever life throws your way without

adverse effects on your health.
Training your brain to manage stress
won't just affect the quality of your
life, but perhaps even the length of it.

Amy Morin

"

It is really wonderful how much
resilience there is in human nature.
Let any obstructing cause, no matter
what, be removed in any way, even

by death, and we fly back to first
principles of hope and enjoyment.

Bram Stoker

I like to use the hard times in the past to motivate me today.

Dwayne "The Rock" Johnson

Enthusiasm is common.
Endurance is rare.

Angela Duckworth

Indeed, this life is a test. It is a test of many things – of our convictions and priorities, our faith and our faithfulness, our patience, and our resilience, and in the end, our ultimate desires.

Sheri L. Dew

If you can't fly then run, if you can't run then walk, if you can't walk then crawl, but whatever you do you have to keep moving forward.

Martin Luther King Jr.

No matter how much falls on us,
we keep ploughing ahead. That's the
only way to keep the roads clear.

Greg Kincaid

Life doesn't get easier or more forgiving;
we get stronger and more resilient.

Steve Maraboli

CHAPTER

6

REFLECTIONS ON RESILIENCE

Resilience isn't a personality trait, it's something that can be nurtured over time, a muscle that can be built. With the right approach and a positive attitude anyone can become more resilient.

Resilience is very different than being numb. Resilience means you experience, you feel, you fail, you hurt. You fall. But, you keep going.

Yasmin Mogahed

Different is good. When someone tells you that you are different, smile and hold your head up and be proud.

Angelina Jolie

Everyone can rise above their
circumstances and achieve success
if they are dedicated to and
passionate about what they do.

Nelson Mandela

Be thankful for the hard times,
for they have made you.

Leonardo DiCaprio

Whether you come from a council estate or a country estate, your success will be determined by your own confidence and fortitude.

Michelle Obama

I know what I can do so it
doesn't bother me what other
people think or their opinion
on the situation.

Usain Bolt

I've missed more than 9,000 shots in my career. I've lost almost 300 games. 26 times, I've been trusted to take the game-winning shot and

missed. I've failed over and over
and over again in my life.
And that's why I succeed.

Michael Jordan

Who cares what people think?
Just believe in yourself.
That's all that matters.

Britney Spears

Rock bottom became the solid
foundation on which I rebuilt my life.

J.K. Rowling

Whenever you have a goal, whether you want to be a doctor or a singer, people will find a way to bring you down. I always tell people that if you have something you're really passionate about, don't let anyone tell you that you can't do it.

Selena Gomez

There are two ways to go when
you hit a crossroads in your life:
There is the bad way, when you
sort of give up, and then there
is the really hard way, when you

fight back. I went the hard way and came out of it ok. Now I'm sitting here and doing great.

Matthew Perry

What would life be if we had no courage to attempt anything?

Gore Vidal

You will have bad times, but
they will always wake you
up to the stuff you weren't
paying attention to.

Robin Williams

"

Life can be much broader once
you discover one simple fact:
Everything around you that you
call life was made up by people
that were no smarter than you.

And you can change it, you can influence it. Once you learn that, you'll never be the same again.

Steve Jobs

Every single thing that I was told that I couldn't do without a label – get in the charts, get on to the Radio 1 playlist – I've done.

Stormzy

Life is not a matter of holding
good cards, but of playing a
poor hand well.

Robert Louis Stevenson

“

The moment we believe that success is determined by an ingrained level of ability as opposed to resilience and hard work, we will be brittle in the face of adversity.

Joshua Waitzkin

Resilience is overcoming adversity,
whilst also potentially changing, or
even dramatically transforming,
(aspects of) that adversity.

Angie Hart

Resilience is accepting your new reality, even if it's less good than the one you had before. You can fight it, you can do nothing but scream about what you've lost, or you can accept that and try to put together something that's good.

Elizabeth Edwards

Resilience is all about being
able to overcome the unexpected.
Sustainability is about survival.
The goal of resilience is to thrive.

Jamais Cascio

Sleep is a key part of the
requirements for resilience
and good decision-making.

James G. Stavridis

Resilience can go
an awful long way.

Eddie the Eagle